T0005128

The Freedom of a Christian

The Crossway Short Classics Series

Heaven Is a World of Love
JONATHAN EDWARDS

The Life of God in the Soul of Man
HENRY SCOUGAL

The Lord's Work in the Lord's Way and No Little People
FRANCIS A. SCHAEFFER

Selected Sermons
LEMUEL HAYNES

THE FREEDOM OF
A CHRISTIAN

A New Translation

MARTIN LUTHER

Translated by Robert Kolb

WHEATON, ILLINOIS

Trade paperback ISBN: 978-1-4335-8226-4
ePub ISBN: 978-1-4335-8229-5
PDF ISBN: 978-1-4335-8227-1
Mobipocket ISBN: 978-1-4335-8228-8

Library of Congress Cataloging-in-Publication Data

Names: Luther, Martin, 1483-1546, author. | Kolb, Robert, 1941- translator.
Title: The freedom of a Christian : a new translation / Martin Luther ; translated by Robert Kolb. Other titles: Tractatus de libertate Christiana. English
Description: Wheaton, Illinois : Crossway, 2023. | Series: Crossway short clasics series | Includes bibliographical references and index.
Identifiers: LCCN 2022012723 (print) | LCCN 2022012724 (ebook) | ISBN 9781433582264 (trade paperback) | ISBN 9781433582271 (pdf) | ISBN 9781433582288 (mobipocket) | ISBN 9781433582295 (epub)
Subjects: LCSH: Liberty—Religious aspects—Christianity.
Classification: LCC BR332.S6 L88 2023 (print) | LCC BR332.S6 (ebook) | DDC 233/.7—dc23/eng/20220714
LC record available at https://lccn.loc.gov/2022012723
LC ebook record available at https://lccn.loc.gov/2022012724

Crossway is a publishing ministry of Good News Publishers.

RRDS   32 31 30 29 28 27 26 25 24 23
14 13 12 11 10 9 8 7 6 5 4 3 2 1

Contents

Foreword

THE YEAR 1520 WAS REMARKABLE for Martin Luther. With the issuing of the papal bull against him, it was becoming clear that there would be no easy and peaceful end to the crisis in Electoral Saxony. And in this context, Luther began to look in two directions. He still hoped against hope that some understanding with Pope Leo X might be possible; and he began to prepare the intellectual framework for a new type of theology. With regard to the latter, he produced three great treatises: *The Babylonian Captivity of the Church*, *An Address to the German Nobility*, and *The Freedom of a Christian*. Taken together, they offer a thoroughgoing manifesto of reform.

The Babylonian Captivity critiqued the medieval sacramental system and proposed an approach that reconfigured baptism and the Mass in clear relation to the prior preached word. The word of God and the believer's grasping of it by faith were the decisive factors in sacramental efficacy. *The Appeal to the German Nobility* offered an ambitious revision of the relationship between church and state, and laid the groundwork for understanding the social and cultural outworking of Luther's approach to salvation. And *The Freedom of a Christian* presented a revised form of Christian ethics—revised, that is, in light of Luther's emerging concept of justification, church, sacraments, culture, politics, and ethics. Luther presented a thoroughgoing example of what reformation in the Saxon key might sound like.

It is the *Freedom* that you have before you. It is a vital text in the Luther canon because it makes clear both how practically different good works are in a Lutheran context—the fruit of forgiveness, not a basis for forgiveness—and the fact that works are still necessary for the believer, a point on which Catholics then and now challenge Protestants. To be forgiven, Luther argues, is to be freed from the law; and the response to freedom from the law is to do good works for one's neighbor as a matter of spontaneous, grateful response. As Christ worked for us, not for his benefit but for ours, so we are called to be "little Christs" to our neighbors—not in the unique, salvific sense that applies only and exclusively to Jesus, but in the sense that our grace toward our neighbors is analogous to his grace toward us. Like Jesus, we do works for our neighbors motivated by love, not by law.

This is something the church must never forget. The Christian life is motivated by the gospel, not by the law. It is the promises of God, and love for God and neighbor, that provide the dynamic for good works. As soon as Christians start to rely on their good works for their standing before God, as soon as they start to do them in order to be right with God, then the character of the Christian life starts to degenerate from that of sons and daughters pleasing their Father to that of servants or employees earning a wage from their boss. And on this, Luther's little essay is excellent, as it is on the importance of the word preached. As Luther makes clear, the conscience is free for good works when the word of promise comes from outside, in its declaration by the preacher. Christians need to be reminded of the promise continually, and that is why we need to be in church and hearing that promise proclaimed.

Readers should remember, of course, that this is an early text from the Reformation Luther. He himself was to discover that a simple focus on the unconditional promise of God could lead to professing Christians, remaining sinful as they do, twisting the very gospel itself into an excuse for evil and then acting in any way they pleased. And to be motivated by love does not necessarily make the content of an action godly or good. That is even truer today, when the concept of love has become little more than a sentiment with little or no moral shape at all. And thus in the late 1520s, Luther wrote his Small Catechism that fleshed out in more detail what works of love might actually look like. But the basic dynamic of Lutheran ethics is here in the 1520 treatise: good works flow from a life justified by faith in the promises of God. And that remains a solid rock on which to build today.

And a final postscript: Let me add that this is not simply a work by my favorite Lutheran theologian of the past. It here appears in an edition produced by my favorite Lutheran theologian and historian of the present, my friend and erstwhile coauthor, Robert Kolb. Bob has trained generations of Lutheran pastors and written books and articles that represent major contributions to our understanding of Luther and his successors. He combines both a profound scholarly knowledge of Lutheran theology and a deep pastoral sensitivity to the needs of Christians today. The reader is in good hands here—that of the dream team of Drs. Luther and Kolb, separated by centuries but united in their common faith. It is a pleasure to commend this edition of a classic to a new generation of Christian readers.

Carl R. Trueman
Professor of Biblical and Religious Studies
Grove City College

Series Preface

JOHN PIPER ONCE WROTE that books do not change people, but paragraphs do. This pithy statement gets close to the idea at the heart of the Crossway Short Classics series: some of the greatest and most powerful Christian messages are also some of the shortest and most accessible. The broad stream of confessional Christianity contains an astonishing wealth of timeless sermons, essays, lectures, and other short pieces of writing. These pieces have challenged, inspired, and borne fruit in the lives of millions of believers across church history and around the globe.

The Crossway Short Classics series seeks to serve two purposes. First, it aims to beautifully preserve these short historic pieces of writing through new high-quality physical editions. Second, it aims to transmit them to a new generation of readers, especially readers who may not be inclined or able to access a larger volume. Short-form content is especially valuable today, as the challenge of focusing in a distracting, constantly moving world becomes more intense. The volumes in the Short Classics series present incisive, gospel-centered grace and truth through a concise, memorable medium. By connecting readers with these accessible works, the Short Classics series hopes to introduce Christians to those great heroes of the faith who wrote them, providing readers with representative works that both nourish the soul and inspire further study.

Readers should note that the spelling and punctuation of these works have been lightly updated where applicable. Scripture references and other citations have also been added where appropriate. Language that reflects a work's origin as a sermon or public address has been retained. Our goal is to preserve as much as possible the authentic text of these classic works. Our prayer is that the Holy Spirit will use these short works to arrest your attention, preach the gospel to your soul, and motivate you to continue exploring the treasure chest of church history, to the praise and glory of God in Christ.

Biography of
Martin Luther

MARTIN LUTHER (1483–1546) was born in
Germany. As a young adult, he was trained for
a theological career within the Roman Catholic
Church. After being caught in a terrifying thun-
derstorm, Luther vowed to God to become a monk.
During his study of the Bible, he plunged into a
period of depression and despair over his sins.
However, everything changed for Luther when he
saw in the Scriptures the doctrine of justification
by faith. Reading "the righteous shall live by faith"
(Rom. 1:17), Luther was freed from his paralyzing

guilt and fear of judgment. "Here I felt that I was altogether born again," he later wrote, "and had entered paradise itself through open gates."[1]

The brilliant Luther committed himself to purifying the medieval church. On October 31, 1517, Luther wrote a letter containing ninety-five theses, or arguments, against various beliefs and practices of the Roman church. Luther insisted that church officials must recover the gospel of grace against ritualistic requirements. The publication of this letter led to the start of the Protestant Reformation, one of the most significant religious movements in world history. Luther's stand for the biblical gospel became a crucial turning point in the story of Western Christianity.

---

1 Martin Luther, *Preface to the Complete Edition of Luther's Latin Writings* in *Career of the Reformer IV*, vol. 34 of *Luther's Works*, ed. Jaroslav Jan Pelikan, Hilton C. Oswald, and Helmut T. Lehmann (Philadelphia: Fortress, 1999), 337.

As the elements of the core of his evangelical theology were coming together, Luther issued a number of treatises in the years 1519 and 1520. Although Luther did not state this, it is likely that he planned to complete the series of treatises calling for reform that he was publishing in those years with a treatise such as *The Freedom of a Christian*. In June 1520, his *On Good Works* set about the reconstruction of the pious life with a treatment of the Ten Commandments that anchored the Christian life in the trust in Christ. That life, he believed, grows out of the first commandment, as he would later paraphrase it in his Small Catechism: "We should fear, love, and trust in God above all things."[2] *On Good Works* was

---

2   Martin Luther, The Small Catechism, in *The Book of Concord: The Confessions of the Evangelical Lutheran Church*, ed. Robert Kolb and Timothy J. Wengert, trans. Charles Arand et al. (Minneapolis: Fortress, 2000), 351.

followed by two works. In the first of these, his *Open Letter to the German Nobility* (August 1520), he deconstructed many ritual practices of medieval piety. Then he critiqued the theological system of dependence on ritual and hierarchy in his *Prelude on the Babylonian Captivity of the Church* (October 1520). That *Prelude* probably pointed to a constructive proposal for Christian life, and that is what he formulated in his *The Freedom of a Christian*, which appeared the next month. He used its Latin version as a plea for understanding to Pope Leo X in the midst of the papal court's preparation of his excommunication. The German is cast in a homiletical form; the Latin takes a formal academic form.

Luther was a prolific writer, authoring hundreds of books, treatises, biblical commentaries, sermons, hymns, and other material. His works have endured for over five hundred years, and many of them are still read widely throughout the Christian world. Throughout his life, Luther emphasized the priesthood of every believer and the sufficiency of Christ's atoning death on the cross to forgive sin and make a person righteous before God. Luther's legacy exists today not only through his timeless writings but also through the hundreds of thousands of Protestant churches throughout the last five centuries.

The text before you is a new translation of the German included and edited in *D. Martin Luthers Werke* (Weimar: Böhlau, 1883–1993), 7:20–38. All content in brackets and footnotes are supplied by the translator. For further comment on the Latin text of the treatise that Luther developed at the same time to his formulating the German text, see Robert Kolb, *Luther's Treatise* On Christian Freedom *and Its Legacy* (Lanham, MD: Lexington Press/Fortress Academic, 2019).

THE FREEDOM OF

A CHRISTIAN

Martin Luther

I

TO THE PERCEPTIVE, wise Hieronymus Mühlphort, electoral administrator of Zwickau,[1] I, Martin Luther, an Augustinian, freely place myself at your service, sir, and wish you all blessings, my special dear friend and patron.[2]

Honorable, wise sir and dear friend:

The worthy Magister Johann Egran, your so praiseworthy municipal preacher,[3] has praised your love and enthusiasm for the Holy Scripture,

---

1 Zwickau was a prominent mining town and commercial center in which the Reformation took hold in the 1520s.

2 This greeting follows the typical form of greeting used by those involved in the educational reform movement labeled "biblical humanism."

3 As was the case with many late medieval towns, the town council paid a municipal preacher since many parish priests were not able to compose sermons.

which you vigorously confess and continually are commending to the people. Therefore, he wanted me to make your acquaintance, and he was able to talk me into doing that; I am most willingly and gladly prepared to do so. For it is a special joy for me to hear that someone loves divine truth since regrettably there are so many, even the majority, who boast about the official title they hold, but who resist the truth with deception and force. As it just is inevitable that many will take offense at Christ, who has been set as a stumbling block and sign for the fall and rising of many [Luke 2:34, Rom. 9:33, 1 Pet. 2:8]. Therefore, in order to launch our relationship and friendship, I have decided to dedicate this little tract and treatise in German to you, which I have written for the pope in Latin, so that for everyone my teaching and writing on the papacy will appear based on something for which

I could not be reproached. I commend myself to you and wish you every kind of divine grace.

Wittenberg, 1520

JESUS

Point 1. I want to set forth two theses so that we may have a fundamental understanding of what a Christian is and what was done [to attain] this freedom that Christ has won for him and given to him, about which Saint Paul has written a good deal:

A Christian is a free lord of everything and subject to no one.

A Christian is a willing servant of everything and subject to everyone.

These two theses are clearly in Saint Paul, 1 Corinthians 9[:19], "I am free in all things and have made myself a servant of everyone," and

Romans 13[:8], "You are to be obligated to no one apart from that you love each other." Love serves and subjects itself to that which it loves. Thus, Paul said also of Christ, Galatians 4[:4], "God sent his Son, born of a woman and made him subject to the law."

Point 2. To take these two contradictory aphorisms regarding freedom and servitude in hand, we should remember that every Christian has two natures, a spiritual nature and a bodily nature. In regard to the soul, a person is called a spiritual, new, inner person, and in regard to flesh and blood is he[4] called a bodily, old, and outward person. And because of the differences between the two, it is said of the Christian in Scripture that

---

4 This translation follows Luther's German literally and refers to all Christians with the singular pronoun in the masculine gender. Luther regarded all Christians, male and female, as equal in God's sight as recipients of his grace and called to the same life of worship and witness.

there are these two opposites, as I said, freedom and servitude.

Point 3. Let us then consider the inner spiritual human being, what his characteristics are, that he is and is called upright, free, a Christian. Thus, it is clear that no outward thing makes him free, or upright, or however it be described, for his uprightness and freedom, likewise his wickedness and bondage, are not external, a matter of the body. What good does it do the soul if the body is not bound, is vigorous and healthy, eats, drinks, lives as it wants to. On the other hand, what does it harm the soul if the body is bound, sick, and exhausted, or is hungry or thirsty or suffering—what no one wants under any conditions. These things do not touch the soul in any way, either to make it free or to make it captive, either to make it upright or to make it wicked.

Point 4. Therefore, it does not help the soul at all if the body wears holy garments, as priests and others in holy orders do, nor does it help if the body is inside the church or in some holy places. Going about its tasks with holy objects provides no special benefit. It makes no difference, either, if a person devotes his body to praying, fasting, a pilgrimage, and all kinds of good works, which may happen through and in the body till the end of time. It must be something completely different that delivers and bestows uprightness and freedom on the soul. For all these things just named, these works and ways, may be performed by a wicked person, a hypocrite and dissembler. Again, it does the soul no harm at all if the body wears clothing that is not holy; is in places that are not holy; eats, drinks, goes on a pilgrimage, or prays, or refrains from all the works that the hypocrite just mentioned performs.

Point 5. The soul has nothing else, neither in heaven nor on earth, in which it lives and is upright, free, and Christian, other than the holy gospel, the word of God proclaimed by Christ. As he himself said in John 11[:25], "I am the life and the resurrection; whoever believes in me lives eternally." So also in John 14[:6], "I am the way, the truth, and the life." Also in Matthew 4[:4], "A person does not live on bread alone but on every word that comes forth from the mouth of God." Therefore, we must be assured that the soul can get along without everything except God's Word, and it finds no help in anything apart from God's word. But when it has the word, it needs nothing else. It has in the word all that it needs: nourishment, joy, peace, light, understanding, righteousness, truth, wisdom, freedom, and everything good in great abundance. Thus, we read in the Psalter, especially in Psalm 119, that the prophet[5] does nothing else than cry out for the word of God. Furthermore, in Scripture the greatest plague and exhibition of God's wrath is considered to be when he withholds his word from human beings [Amos 8:11–12]. On the other hand, there is no greater grace than when he sends his word, as Psalm 107[:20] states, "He sent forth his word in order to provide help." And Christ has come to fulfill no other task than to proclaim the word of God. Also all apostles, bishops, priests, and the entire clerical walk of life are called and placed in office only because of the word, although things are moving rapidly in the opposite direction [in our time].

Point 6. You ask, "Which is this word that bestows such great grace, and how shall I use it?"

---

5   Luther regarded David not only as a king and a psalmist but also as a prophet, who with his psalms had proclaimed God's word to Israel.

Answer: It is nothing other than the proclamation that Christ delivered [sinners], as contained in the gospel, in which you are to hear your God speaking to you, what has to be and what has been done. [It tells you] that your entire life and all you do is nothing in God's sight but you on your own way to eternal ruin with everything in you. If you really believe that, that you are guilty, you must despair of yourself and confess that what Hosea said is true: "O Israel, in you is nothing other than ruin. Only in me is there any help for you" [Hos. 13:9]. In order for you to get away from yourself, that is, from your ruin, he places before you his dear Son Jesus Christ and has him say to you through his living word of comfort that you are to give yourself to him in firm faith and brashly trust in him. In this way, for the sake of this very faith, your sins are forgiven, your entire ruin is overcome, and you are righteous, faithful, set at peace, upright, and have fulfilled all the commandments. You are free from all things. As Saint Paul says in Romans 1[:17], "A justified Christian lives only by faith," and Romans 10[:4], "Christ is the end and the fulfillment of all the commandments for all who believe in him."

Point 7. Therefore, it is proper that the only activity and effort of every Christian is to mold the image of the word and Christ into his heart, and continually practice and strengthen this faith. For no other activity produces a Christian. It is as Christ said to the Jews in John 6[:28–29], when they asked what kind of activity they should perform to be doing something godly and Christian. He said, "This is the only godly activity, that you believe in him whom God has sent," the only one whom the Father has appointed. Therefore, it is indeed a treasure overflowing to have true faith in Christ, for faith brings with it all blessing and takes away all misfortune. As it states in the last chapter of Mark [16:16], "Whoever believes and is baptized will be saved. Whoever does not believe will be damned." Therefore, the prophet in Isaiah 10[:22] saw what a treasure this faith is and said, "God will make a speedy reckoning on earth, and this reckoning will, like a deluge, gush out righteousness"—that is, faith, for therein all the commandments are simply fulfilled. It will bestow righteousness in abundance on all who have this faith so that they need nothing more to be righteous and upright. Thus Saint Paul says in Romans 10[:10] that the fact that "a person believes from the heart makes him righteous and upright."

Point 8. How does it happen that faith alone makes a person upright and lavishly bestows riches when in Scripture there is so much prescribed by the law, by the commandments, by the works we are to do, by our responsibilities in life, and by directions for the ways we are to act? Here one must note carefully and continually consider seriously that only faith apart from all works makes one upright, free, and blessed, as we will hear more later. And one must also know that the entire Holy Scripture is divided into two kinds of the word, which are command or God's law and promises or words of assurance. The commands teach and prescribe various kinds of good works, but having them prescribed does not make them happen. They certainly give direction but do not provide assistance; they teach what a person should do but do not give any power at all to do these things. Therefore, they have been established to let people see their inability to perform the good and learn to despair of themselves. Therefore, they are called the old testament and belong all to the old testament.[6] For example, the command "you are not to have evil desires" [i.e., covet; Ex. 20:17] proves that we are completely sinners and that no one is able to exist without evil desires, try as hard as a person wants to try. From this he learns to despair of himself and to seek help somewhere else so that he can get rid of the evil desires and thus fulfill through another person what he cannot do himself. Likewise, all the other commandments are impossible for us.

Point 9. When a person has learned and sensed from the commandments that he is not capable of fulfilling the law, this only causes him to worry about how he can satisfy the law, since the command must be fulfilled, or he must be damned. Then he is truly humbled and reduced to nothing

---

6   At this point, Luther is using the term "old testament" as a synonym for the law of God as given to Moses, not as a designation for the time before Christ.

in his own eyes, finding nothing in himself by which he might become upright. Then comes the other word, the divine promise and assurance, and says, "If you wish to fulfill all the commandments, lay aside your evil desires, and get rid of your sin, as the commandments require and demand, then look, believe in Christ, in whom I give you assurance of all grace, righteousness, peace, and freedom. If you believe that, you have it; if you do not believe it, you do not have it. For it is impossible for you [to attain it] through all the works of the commandments, but that will be easy and simple for you through faith. For I have placed all things in compact form in faith, so that whoever has faith is to have all things and be saved, but whoever does not have faith is to have nothing." Therefore, the promise from God bestows what the commandments demand, and it accomplishes what the commandments intend to do, that all may belong to God. Command and fulfillment: he alone commands them; he alone fulfills them. Therefore, this promise is God's word of the new testament and belongs in the new testament.

Point 10. This and every word of God is holy, reliable, righteous, peace-giving, liberating, and full of all goodness. Therefore, whoever clings to it with true faith will bring the soul into harmony with him so that all the virtues of the word will become property of the soul. Through faith, the soul will become holy, righteous, faithful, at peace, free, and full of all goodness, a true child of God, as [stated in] John 1[:12], "He gave them the power to become children of God who believe in his name."

From this it is easy to note why faith is able to do so much and that no good work is capable of doing the same thing. For no good work hangs on the divine word, as faith does. Good works cannot be in the soul, but only the word and faith reign in the soul. As this word [of the promise in Christ] is, so will the soul be from that word, just as iron becomes red hot as fire by being united with fire. Thus, we see that in faith a Christian has enough, needs no works to be upright. If he cannot rely on works any longer, he is released from commandments and laws. If he is released, he is certainly free. Such is Christian freedom. It is not that faith alone creates a situation in which we may plunge into idleness or may do evil works but that we do not need works to attain uprightness and salvation. On this we intend to say more later.

II

Point 11. To take this a little further, with faith it happens that when one person believes the other, he believes him because he regards him as an upright, reliable person. That is the greatest honor that one human being can give another, just as it is the most shameful thing when one person regards another as a scoundrel, a liar, a wanton person. Therefore, when the soul firmly trusts God's word, it regards him as reliable, upright, and righteous, and it gives the greatest of all honors that can be given to him. It acknowledges his righteousness, it honors his name, and it lets him act as he wishes, for it does not doubt that he is upright, reliable in his every word. On the other hand, a person can dishonor God in no greater fashion than not to trust him, so that the soul regards him as insufficient, deceptive, and unreliable, and to the greatest extent possible denies him with such mistrust. It sets up an idol according to its own imagination in the heart, in opposition to God, as though it knows better than God. When God sees that the soul acknowledges his reliability and thus honors him with its trust, God honors the soul and regards it as upright and faithful, and the soul is upright and faithful through this faith. For a person thus acknowledges God's faithfulness and uprightness, that he is righteous and true and acts righteously and reliably. For it is true and proper to acknowledge that God will give the truth. That is what such people do not do when they do not believe even though they strive and weary themselves with many good works.

Point 12. Not only does faith bestow so much that the soul, like the divine word, is filled with grace and is free and blessed. But the soul is also united with Christ as a bride with her bridegroom. The result of this marriage, as Saint Paul says [Eph. 5:30], is that Christ and the soul are one body, and therefore they hold everything they possess, the good and the bad and all things, in common. What Christ possesses belongs to the believing soul, and what the soul has belongs to Christ. So if Christ has all good things and blessedness, they also belong to the soul. If the soul has all vice and sin, they become Christ's possession. This takes place as a joyous exchange and encounter. Because Christ is God and a human being who has never sinned and because his upright character is unassailable, eternal, and almighty, he takes possession of the sin of the believing soul with her bridal ring, which is faith, and he acts in no other way than that he himself had committed the sin. Thus, the sin must be devoured and drowned by him. For his unassailable righteousness is too strong. Thus, the soul is free and cleared of all sin for the sake of faith, simply because of the betrothal gift from the bridegroom— that is, because of faith—and the soul is given the eternal righteousness of her bridegroom,

Christ. Is that not a joyous transaction, when the rich, noble, upright bridegroom Christ takes the poor, contemptible, evil little whore in marriage and takes away all the evil she has and adorns her with every good thing? So it is not possible that sin condemns her, for she lies now on Christ and is consumed by him. Thus, she has true righteousness in her bridegroom, so that she can stand against all sin, although the sins certainly lie upon her.[7] Paul speaks of this in 1 Corinthians 15[:57, 54]: "Thanks and praise to God, who has given us such a victory in Christ Jesus, in whom death is swallowed up along with sin."

Point 13. Here you see on what basis so much is properly ascribed to faith, that it fulfills all the

---

7   This sort of bridal imagery can be traced back to the sermons of Bernard of Clairvaux (1090–1153), Luther's favorite medieval theologian, and it was prominent in the monastic-mystical piety of fifteenth-century German-speaking lands.

commandments, and without any other works
it renders a person upright. For here you see that
faith by itself fulfills the first commandment,
where it is commanded, "You are to honor one
God" [Ex. 20:2-3].[8] If you were nothing but good
works from head to toe, you still would not prove
that you are upright and be offering God the
honor due him, and therefore you would not be
fulfilling the first commandment. For God does
not want to be honored unless he is being cred-
ited with being reliable and [the source of] every
good thing, as he truly is. Therefore, faith alone is
the righteousness of a person and the fulfillment
of all the commandments. For whoever fulfills
the first, the chief, commandment certainly and
easily fulfills the other commandments. Works

---

8   This emphasis on the first commandment develops the chief
    argument of Luther's *On Good Works*, published some five
    months before *The Freedom of a Christian*.

are dead objects. They cannot honor or praise God, although they may be performed in such way that they honor God and praise him. But we are seeking here that which is not done as a work but is that which performs the works, the master that produces them. That is what honors God and performs the works. That is nothing else but faith in the heart, which is the chief, indeed the entire, essence of being upright. Therefore, it is a risky, obscure expression to teach that God's commandments are fulfilled by works, for the fulfillment of all works must take place through faith, and works follow faith's fulfillment, as we will hear.

Point 14. To look further at what we have in Christ and what a great blessing true faith is, one must know that before the Old Testament[9] and in it God set aside and reserved for himself all the

---

9   At this point, "Old Testament" does refer to the time before Christ and God's relationship with the Hebrew people in that time.

firstborn of human beings and of animals [Exod. 13:12]. The firstborn was highly prized and had two great advantages over all the other children, the positions of master and priest, or the offices of king and priest. That means that in earthly affairs the firstborn male child was a lord over all his brothers and a parson or pope in relation to God. What is signified by this figure[10] is Jesus Christ. He himself is indeed the firstborn male child of God the Father through the virgin Mary. Therefore, he is a king and a priest, spiritually, for his kingdom is not earthly nor a matter of what is earthly, but it has to do with spiritual blessings, such as his faithfulness, wisdom, peace, joy, blessedness, etc. However, that does not exclude

10 The German *Figur* represents the Latin concept of *figura*, a form of expression closely related to "type," here an Old Testament historical event that prophesied of Jesus Christ or the church and the life of the believer.

temporal blessings, for everything in heaven, on earth, and in hell is subjected to him, although one does not see him, which means that he rules spiritually and invisibly.

Therefore, his priesthood is not constituted by outward gesticulations or clothing, as we see among human beings, but it is constituted by the spiritual, the invisible—namely, that he continually represents his own before God and sacrifices himself and does everything that a proper priest is supposed to do. He makes intercession for us, as Saint Paul says in Romans 8[:34]. In this he also teaches us inwardly in our hearts. These are the two truly proper tasks of a priest. In the same way, human priests on earth, in time, make intercession and teach.

Point 15. What Christ the firstborn has in honor and dignity he shares with all his Christians that through their faith they may also be kings and priests with Christ, as Saint Peter says, 1 Peter 2[:9]: "You are a priestly kingdom and a kingly priesthood." And so it is that a Christian is raised high above all things so that he is a lord of all things spiritually, for nothing can harm him in regard to salvation. Indeed, everything has to be subject to him and be of help for his salvation, as Saint Paul teaches in Romans 8[:28]: "All things must contribute to the best for the elect," whether it be life, death, sin, uprightness, good and evil, whatever it can be called. Likewise, in 1 Corinthians 3[:21–22], "All things are yours, whether life or death, present or future, etc." Not that we exercise power in a physical sense over everything, either in possession or in use, as earthly human beings, for our bodies must die, and no one can escape death. In the same way, we are subject to many other things, as we see in Christ and his saints. For this is a spiritual lordship, which reigns even when oppressed in regard to the body. That is, apart from everything else it finds benefit in regard to my soul, that even death and suffering must serve me and become of use for my salvation. That is indeed a high and honorable dignity and a truly almighty lordship, a spiritual kingdom, since nothing is so good, so evil, that it does not have to serve me to my advantage. Thus, I believe, and I need absolutely nothing else. On the contrary, my faith is sufficient for me. Just see what a precious freedom and power Christians possess!

Point 16. Beyond that, we are priests—that is, we are much more than just a king, for the priesthood makes us worthy to come into God's presence and intercede for others. To stand before God is the task of no one other than the priest. Therefore, Christ has made us his own so that we may spiritually enter into God's presence and intercede for another person, just as priests entered into God's presence physically and interceded for the people. Nothing works for the good of anyone who does not believe in Christ. Such a person is a slave to all things and must be aggravated by everything. The prayer of this kind of person is not pleasing to God and does not come into the presence of God. Who could even imagine the honor and exalted status of a Christian? His kingship grants him power over all things. His priesthood grants him power over God, for God does what he asks and wishes, as it is written in the Psalms, "God does the will of those who fear him, and he hears their prayer" [Ps. 145:19]. To such an honor they come only through faith. From that, it is clearly seen how a Christian is free from all things and is over all things, and thus he needs no good works in order to be upright and blessed. Instead, faith brings him everything in great abundance. And if such a person were so foolish and thought that by a good work a person becomes upright, free, saved, or Christian, he would have lost faith and everything along with it, just like the dog that is carrying a piece of meat in its mouth and snaps at the reflection in the water, thereby losing both the meat and its reflection.

Point 17. You may be asking, "What is the difference between a priest and a lay person in Christendom if they are all priests?" The answer is, "The little word 'priest,' 'parson,' 'cleric,' and the like is misused if it is taken away from the common people and attributed to a small group that is called the spiritual estate. Holy Scripture makes no other difference other than that the learned and consecrated are called in Latin, *ministros, servos, oeconomos*—that is, servant, bondsman, steward, who are to proclaim faith and Christian freedom to the other Christians. For although we are all priests on the same level, not all can serve [in this office] or administer [the sacraments] or preach. Therefore, Saint Paul says, 1 Corinthians 4[:1], "We do not wish to be regarded as anything more by other people than as Christ's servants and stewards of the gospel." In our day, there has developed from this post as steward such a temporal, external, opulent, fearsome lordship and power that can in no way be compared to the properly exercised temporal exercise of power, [acting as if] the lay people were something other than Christians. With that, the entire Christian understanding of grace, freedom, faith, and everything we have in Christ, even Christ himself, is taken away. In their place we have many human laws and works, and become subjugated completely to the most incompetent people on earth.[11]

---

11 Luther often deplored the lack of education and understanding of many of the clergy. Many priests had little or no formal training in theology, and some no university education at all.

Point 18. From all this, we learn that it is not enough when the life and work of Christ has been proclaimed in a cursory manner and only as history, as a historical chronicle of events, not to mention if nothing is said of Christ and only canon law or other human laws and doctrines are proclaimed. There are also many who preach or lecture on Christ, showing much sympathy for him, or expressing anger against the Jews, or even more childish kinds of things. But if he is to be preached, he must be preached, in a manner that faith is aroused and is sustained in you and me. This faith awakes and is retained when I am told why Christ has come, how a person is to make use of his coming and how to benefit from him, what he has brought me and given me. That takes place where someone correctly sets forth Christian freedom, the freedom we have from Christ, and that we are kings and priests, powerful in all things, and that all that we do is pleasing to God and God hears it, as I have said up to this point. For when a heart listens to Christ, it must rejoice from its very foundation, find comfort, and in tenderness be turned to Christ to love him once again. To such a situation [filled] with laws or works, a person should never again want to return. For who would intend to damage and terrorize such a heart? When sin and death fall away, the heart believes that Christ is its uprightness, and its sin never again belongs to it but belongs to Christ. Therefore, sin must disappear in the face of Christ's uprightness in faith, as was said above, and the heart learns with the apostle to act defiantly toward death and sin and say, "Where is now your victory, O death? Where is now, death, your stinger? Your stinger is sin. But God be praised and thanked, who has given us the victory through Jesus Christ our Lord. And death has been swallowed up in his victory, etc." [1 Cor. 15:55–57, 54].

Point 19. That is enough said about the inner person, about its freedom and its core righteousness, which needs no law or good works, for indeed they are harmful for it if a person has the presumption that he can become righteous through them. Here we want to answer all those who take offense at what has been said and are accustomed to say, "Oh, so then, if faith is everything and suffices alone to make a person upright, why are good works commanded? We want to live it up and do nothing." No, dear fellow, that is not the way it is. It would be so if you were only a person with an inner being and totally spiritual and inward, which will not be the case until the last day. There is and remains on earth only a beginning and growth, which will be completed in the future world. This is what the apostle calls the *primatias spiritus* [Rom. 8:23]—that is, the firstfruits of the Spirit—and therefore at this point belongs to what was said above: "a Christian is a willing servant of everything and is subject to everyone." At the same time that he is free and needs to do nothing, he is a servant and must do everything. We want now to see how that fits together.

III

Point 20. Although the person inwardly, in the soul, is perfectly justified through faith and has everything that he should have—apart from the fact that this faith and grace must always be on the increase until he comes into the future life—he remains on this earth in his bodily existence and must keep his own body under control and interact with other people. This is where works come in, and he must not be indolent in this regard. Indeed, the body must be restrained and trained with fasting, vigils, working, and all reasonable discipline so that it is obedient to and conforms to the inner person and faith, so that it does not hinder or resist, as it is prone to do when it is not coerced. For the inward person is one with God, joyous and exuberant for the sake of Christ, who has done so much for him. Thus, this inner person desires nothing else but that it might serve God in a free body without thought of reward. Therefore, it finds in its flesh a rebellious will, which wants to serve the world and is looking for what pleases it. Faith cannot tolerate this and gladly goes for its jugular vein in order to suppress it and defend against it, as Saint Paul says, Romans 7[:22–23], "I delight in God's will in my inward person, but I find another will in my flesh, which wants to take me captive through sin." Likewise, "I discipline my body and drive it to obedience so that I have nothing in myself that is reproachable since I am to teach others" [1 Cor. 9:27]. Likewise, Galatians 5[:24]: "All who belong to Christ crucify their flesh with its evil desires."

Point 21. But precisely these works dare not be performed with the idea that through them a human being becomes upright in God's sight, for faith cannot abide this false idea. Faith is and must be our uprightness in God's sight, but that includes recognizing that the body becomes obedient and purified from its evil desires and that the eye looks at these evil desires only to drive them out. For because the soul is pure through faith and loves God, it ardently desires that everything be pure, above all its own body, and everyone loves and praises God with the soul. So it happens that the human being cannot be indolent for the sake of his own body and must do many good works above and beyond so that he keeps it under control. To be sure, the works are not the proper stuff from which a person becomes upright and righteous in God's sight, but he does them with no thought of gain, out of uncoerced love, in order to please God. He seeks in them nothing else, nor does he see anything else in them than that they are pleasing to God, for whose sake he gladly does everything at the very best level. From this, each person can himself make a proper estimation and assessment of how to control the body. Such a person fasts, keeps a vigil, exerts himself as much as he sees is necessary for the body to suppress its willfulness. The others, who think that with works they can become upright, pay no attention to such discipline but are looking only at their works. They are thinking that if they only do many and important works, it will be well with them, and they will become upright. At times, they break their heads and ruin their bodies in this effort. That is a huge foolishness and misunderstanding of the Christian life and faith, that they want to become upright and be saved apart from faith through works.

Point 22. To offer an analogy: One should not view the works of a Christian, who through faith and by the pure grace of God without hope of reward is righteous and is saved, in any other way than as if they were the works of Adam and Eve in paradise. Of them it is written in Genesis 2[:15], "God placed the human being he had created in paradise so that he might work it and take care of it." Adam was created by God upright and at peace, without sin. Adam certainly did not become upright and righteous by his work and care of the garden. But in order that he not be indolent, God gave him something to do, to plant paradise, to cultivate it, and to watch over it. That was work completely freely given, not for the sake of any gain, but simply to do what pleases God and not thereby to attain uprightness. He already had that uprightness; it would have been inborn in us all by nature. In like manner, the works of a believer, which are performed by faith, place a person once again in paradise. Such a person is a new creation, who needs no works to become upright. But at the same time he dare not be indolent and must discipline and take care of his body. Such freely performed works, done only to do what is pleasing to God, are [what is] commanded.

Likewise, just as an ordained bishop, when he consecrates a church, confirms children, or does some other task as part of his office, is not made a bishop by doing these works. No, if he had not been ordained a bishop already, his works would have no validity and would be nothing more than the work of a fool. Therefore, a Christian, who is consecrated by faith, does good works and does not become better or more consecrated (nothing other than faith can give that kind of growth) as a Christian. Otherwise, all his works would be nothing other than simply foolish, blameworthy, damnable sins.

Point 23. Therefore, these two statements are true: "Good, upright works never produce a good upright person, but a good, upright person produces good, upright works. Evil works never produce an evil person, but an evil person produces evil works." Therefore, the person must be good and upright before there are any good works, and good works follow and are the result of the person's being good and upright. Just as Christ said, "A bad tree does not bear good fruit. A good tree bears no bad fruit" [Matt. 7:18]. It is clear that the fruit does not bear the tree, and trees do not grow on fruit, but the tree produces the fruit, and the fruit grow on the trees. The tree is there before the fruit, and the fruit do not make the tree good or bad, but the tree makes the fruit. Therefore, the human being must be in his person upright or evil before he does good or evil works. But his works do not make him good or evil; instead, he performs good or evil works. We see the same in all the trades. A good or bad house does not make a good or bad carpenter, but a good or bad carpenter makes a bad or a good house. No work makes its craftsman once the work exists. Instead, as is the one who makes something, so the product. Thus, whether a person is in faith or unbelief determines the nature of the work of a person, whether it is good or bad. It is not, again, that what he produces determines whether he is upright and believing. Just as their works do not make them believers, so their works also do not make them upright in their behavior. But just as faith makes a person upright, so it also produces good works. Thus, works do not make a person upright, and the person must be upright before he does the work. Thus, it is clear that only faith, on the basis of pure grace through Christ and his word, makes a person completely upright and saves him. No work, no command is necessary for a Christian for salvation, but the Christian is free from all commands. On the basis of pure freedom, without any thought of gain, he does everything that he does, seeking neither benefit nor salvation. For he already has everything that he needs and is saved through his faith and God's grace. No, indeed, he wants only to do what is pleasing to God.

Point 24. On the other hand, for the person without faith, there is no good work that benefits him or saves him. By contrast, no evil work makes a person evil and damns him. Unbelief does that.

It makes the person and the tree bad. Such a person does evil and damnable works. Therefore, the good or evil state of a person does not begin with the performance of works but with faith. As the Wise One [Jesus ben Sirach, the author of the intertestamental book bearing his name, written in the second century BC] said, "The beginning of every sin is departing from God and not trusting him" [Jesus Sirach 10:14–15].[12] Likewise, Christ taught that one should not begin by looking at the works. He said, "Either make the tree good and its fruit will be good, or make the tree bad, and its fruit will be bad," as though he was say-

---

12 Luther followed the canonical qualifications of Saint Jerome (ca. 345–420), which included placing the apocryphal books in a secondary category as books extant only in Greek. He wrote in his German Bible of 1534 that these books are "not regarded as equal to the Holy Scripture and are nonetheless useful and good to read." The Wisdom of Jesus Sirach was the most frequently used of the Apocrypha among Luther's students because of its helpful moral instruction.

ing, "Whoever wants to have good fruit must first begin with the tree and plant a good tree" [Matt. 12:33]. Therefore, whoever wants to do good works must not look first at the works but at the person who is to do the works. No one makes the person good; only faith does that, and nothing makes a person evil apart from unbelief. It is true indeed that works make a person upright or evil in the eyes of other human beings—that is, they show outwardly who is upright or evil. As Christ says, Matthew 7[:20], "By their fruit you shall know them." But that is all the outward appearance. This outward manifestation leads many astray; they write and teach how a person should do good works and become upright, and they never give faith a thought. They go their own way, and one blind person is leading another. They torture themselves with many works and never strive to be genuinely upright. Of them Saint Paul says,

2 Timothy 3[:5–7], "They have the appearance of being upright, but there is no foundation under them. They go forth and are continually learning and never come to a knowledge of true uprightness." Whoever does not want to wander off with these blind teachers must look further than to works, commands, or the teaching of works. Such a person must look at the person above all else, how people become upright. That kind of person does not receive salvation and become upright through commands and works, but through the word of God (that is, through the promise of grace) and through faith. God's honor consists in this: that he does not save us through our works but by his gracious word, given without condition and out of pure mercy.

Point 25. From all this it is easy to understand in what way we are to set aside good works and in what way we are not to set aside good works and how to understand all instruction that teaches good works. For where the false attachment [of works to the salvation of sinners] and a perverse interpretation is present—that through works we should become upright and find salvation—the works are already not properly performed but instead damning. For they are not freely performed, and they dishonor God's grace, which makes people upright and saves them only through faith. Works are not capable of doing that, but they tried to strive to make that work and grab away from grace what it does and its honor. Therefore, we do not reject good works because of what they are in themselves but because of this wicked application of them [to the way of salvation] and false, perverse interpretations of them. These interpretations make it so that they only appear to be good and in fact are not good, deceiving oneself and everyone else, just as the ravenous wolf in sheep's clothing [Matt. 7:15]. This wicked association of works with salvation and such muddled interpretations are not to be overcome where there is no faith. It has to be so with those who seek their own holiness through their works until faith comes and destroys all this, which nature cannot drive out of them on its own.[13] Indeed, they cannot recognize it, but they regard this association of works with salvation as a precious blessing. Therefore, so many are deceived by this opinion. For this reason, although it is good to write and preach of remorse, confession of sins, satisfaction, if a person does not go further than that, to faith, it is certainly simply devilish, deceptive teaching. A person dare not preach one or the other alone but both

13   This reflects Luther's conviction that the human will is bound to choose idols, including its own performance of good works, over the true God until it is liberated from sin.

words of God. The command is to be preached to terrify the sinners and to reveal their sins, so that they feel remorse and repent. But that is not where the matter should end. The other word has to be preached, the assurance of grace, in order to teach faith. Without faith, the command, remorse, and everything else is in vain. There still are preachers who preach remorse, sin, and grace, but they do not explain in detail either the commandments or the promise of God in a way that teaches from where remorse and grace come. For remorse flows out of the commandments, faith out of the promises of God. Therefore, a person is justified and raised up by faith in the divine word after being humbled by fear of God's commands and coming to know him.

Point 26. This has been said of works in general and the discipline of the Christian's own body.

Now we want to discuss more works which the Christian performs for other people. A person does not live alone in this physical existence but lives in the midst of other human beings on earth. Therefore, no one can exist without doing works for others. He must always be speaking with another person and has to deal with others, even though these works are not necessary for him to be upright and saved. Therefore, he should think freely about all his works and direct them only to the service and benefit of others. There is no other pattern for him apart from what the other person needs. That is then a truly Christian life, and faith goes to work with enthusiasm and love, as Saint Paul teaches the Galatians [5:6]. In Philippians [2:1–4], he taught them how they had complete grace and everything they needed through their faith in Christ. He taught them further and said,

I admonish you on the basis of all the comfort which you have in Christ, and all the comfort which you have in our love for you, and in all the fellowship that you have with all spiritual upright Christians. If you want to make my heart rejoice perfectly, from now on, share the same way of thinking and show love to one another, serve one another, and each one pay attention not to himself or his own things, but to others and what they need.

You see that Paul clearly defines the Christian life as a life directed toward all good works for the benefit of the neighbor. Because every Christian has enough for himself [to be saved] in his own faith, and all other works and life are his, he serves the neighbor out of a freely given love. Paul adds Christ to that as an example and says, "Have the same way of thinking that you see in

Christ." Although he was fully in the form of God and was complete in himself, and an earthly life, activities, and suffering were not necessary for him to become upright and gain salvation, he nevertheless emptied himself and acted as a servant, did all that had to be done and suffered, considering nothing else than what is best for us, and therefore although he was free, he became a servant for our sakes [Phil. 2:5–8].

Point 27. Therefore, a Christian, like Christ, his head, is full and satiated, and should be content with his faith, and always be cultivating it, for it is his life, his uprightness, his salvation. It gives him everything that God and Christ has,[14] as is mentioned above. And Saint Paul in Galatians 2[:20], "What I am still living in the body, I am living in faith in Christ,

---

14 Here Luther uses the singular verb for the plural subject "God and Christ."

God's Son." Although he is completely free, he willingly makes himself a servant in order to help his neighbor, to deal with him and treat him as God has dealt with him through Christ, and to do that with no thought of gain, seeking nothing other than to do what is pleasing to God. He thinks, "Well, just look! Through and in Christ, my God has given me, an unworthy, condemned person, apart from any merit, totally unconditionally out of pure mercy, the riches of complete uprightness and salvation so that I henceforth need nothing but faith, and that is the way it is. Indeed, for such a Father, who has poured out upon me his overabundant blessings, I want to do what is pleasing to him freely, joyfully, and without thought of reward. I want to be a Christ for my neighbor, as Christ has been for me. I want to do nothing other than that which I see my neighbor needs, what is useful for him and is a blessing for him, because I have in Christ all that is sufficient for me through faith." Thus you see how love and enthusiasm flow from faith in God, and out of this love flows a free, willing, joyous life in serving the neighbor without thought of reward. For just as our neighbor suffers great privation and needs whatever we can give him, so we were suffering great need in relationship to God and required his grace. Therefore, as God has helped us through Christ unconditionally, so we should do nothing else with our bodies and its actions than help our neighbor. Thus, we see that what an exalted and noble life it is to live as a Christian. Unfortunately, that is not only not to be found in the whole world, but it is no longer confessed or proclaimed.

Point 28. Thus, we read in Luke 2[:22–38] that the Virgin Mary went to the church after six weeks and went through purification rites according to the law, as all other women did, even though she did not become unclean through [the birth of] Christ and thus was not obligated to go through the purification and did not need to do this. But she did it freely out of love so that she would not show contempt for other women but would remain [on the same level] with the other mothers. Likewise, Saint Paul had Saint Timothy circumcised even though it was not necessary [Acts 16:3]. He did it so that he would not give the Jews who were weak in faith a reason to think evil thoughts, although in a similar situation he did not let Titus be circumcised because some were pressing that he had to be circumcised and that this was necessary for salvation [Gal. 2:3]. And similarly, Christ in Matthew 17[:24–27]: When he was asked for a penny for the tax, he posed the question to Saint Peter whether the king's children were not free from paying the tax. Saint Peter said "yes," and Christ told him to go to the sea and said, "So that we do not give offense to them, go there and take the first fish you catch, and in its mouth you will find a penny. Pay that for me and for you." That is a fine example of this teaching, in that Christ calls himself and his disciples free children of the King, who need nothing, and in spite of that he submits willingly, serves, and pays the tax. Just as doing this was not necessary for Christ to do and did not contribute to his uprightness or blessedness, so all his other works and the works of his Christians are not necessary for salvation, but they are all freely given service for the sake of others and to enhance their lives. Therefore, all of the works of priests, monasteries, and ecclesiastical foundations should be done for the same reason that all people in their own walks of life and in the places where God created him are to do works only for the welfare of others and for disciplining their own bodies, to give others an example to do the same, for they need to discipline the body. But indeed they always should be careful that they do not undertake such works in order to become upright and win salvation. That is possible only through faith. For these reasons, Saint Paul commands in Romans 13[:1–7] and Titus 3[:1–2] that they be subject to temporal powers and be prepared, not so that they become upright through this but that they freely serve others and governmental authority, and do what they want out of love and freedom. Whoever understands this can easily find the proper direction to go in the midst of the countless commands and laws of the pope, the bishops, the monasteries, the ecclesiastical foundations, the princes and lords, which some mad prelates also promote as if they were necessary for salvation, contending that they are to be called commands of the church, indeed improperly. For a free Christian says, "I want to fast, pray, do this and that that is commanded, not because I need it or want to be upright and gain salvation through it. Instead, for the sake of the pope, bishops, the community, my fellow human beings, I want to give an example to them to serve them and suffer [on their behalf], just as Christ has acted and suffered many greater things for my welfare, things that were far less necessary for him. And even if the tyrants practice injustice when they make such demands, [carrying out these unjust but not ungodly commands] does not harm me because it is not against God."

Point 29. From this, every person may gain a certain estimate and [be able to make a] distinction among all works and commands, even between those that are from blind, mad [prelates], and from rightly thinking prelates. For whatever work is not directed toward serving others or suffering in submission to another person's will (in so far as it does not force a person to act against God) is not a good Christian work. That is why I am worried that few foundation churches,[15] monasteries, altars, Masses, and dispositions of inheritance are Christian. The same thing goes for the fasting and prayers that are performed, especially for certain saints. For I fear that in all of these activities each person is only seeking his own benefit by thinking that he can in this way perform repentance for his sin and gain salvation. All this comes from ignorance of

---

15 Foundation churches were not formally part of the monastic system—that is, they did not belong to an established order—but were churches endowed by a donor and staffed with canons who adhered to the monastic discipline and were dedicated to saying Masses for the departed.

faith and Christian freedom. Some blind prelates drive people to do this and praise this sort of thing, and adorn them with indulgences and do not teach faith at all anymore. I advise you, however, if you want to offer a donation, pray, or fast, do not do it thinking that you want to have some benefit for yourself, but give it freely so that other people may enjoy what you give. When you do it for their good, then you are a true Christian. What can your material goods and your good works that are left for you to discipline your body and provide for it do for you? You have enough in faith, in which God has given you all things, do you not? Behold, God's blessings must flow from one person to others and be shared so that every person accept his neighbor as if the neighbor were himself. From Christ these blessings flow to us, for he has taken all that belongs to us into his life, as if he were the very person who we are. From us they should flow to those who need them. It is even so that I must place my faith and righteousness before God in behalf of my neighbor, cover his sins, take them onto myself, and do nothing else than act as if they are my own, just as Christ has done for us all. That is the nature of love when it is truly love. It is genuine where faith is genuine. Therefore, the holy apostle characterized love, 1 Corinthians 13[:5], by writing that "it does not seek its own but what is for the neighbor."

Point 30. From all of this comes the conclusion that a Christian lives not in himself but in Christ and in his neighbor, in Christ through faith, in the neighbor through love. Through faith he rises above himself in God, from God he descends under himself through love, and remains always in God and in divine love. It is as Christ said in John 1[:51]: "You will see heaven standing open and the angels ascending and descending over the Son of Man." Behold, that is the proper, spiritual Christian freedom, which liberates the heart from all sins, laws, and commands. This freedom exceeds all other freedoms, as high as heaven is over the earth. May God grant us that we truly understand that and retain it. Amen.

Scripture Index

CROSSWAY SHORT
CLASSICS

FOR MORE INFORMATION, VISIT **CROSSWAY.ORG**.